DE LA 5e À LA 4e
12 • 13 ANS

Operation Blue Lagoon

CHARLOTTE GARNER
écrivain

JACQUES MARCELIN
agrégé d'anglais

illustré par
DOMINIQUE HÉ

Le papier de cet ouvrage est composé de fibres naturelles, renouvelables, fabriquées à partir de bois provenant de forêts gérées de manière responsable.

Nathan

Présentation

Lire un récit d'aventure en anglais
entrecoupé d'exercices de :
- compréhension (corrigés à la fin de chaque chapitre).
- grammaire.

→ S'aider de la traduction :
- des mots difficiles signalés par un astérisque* ;
- des verbes au prétérit irrégulier, signalés par un numéro (voir la liste page 94).

→ Résoudre des exercices
qui permettent de reconstituer l'histoire.

→ Vérifier sa réponse :
- elle est juste → suite de l'histoire ;
- elle est fausse → le corrigé guide pour refaire l'exercice.

→ Consulter le mémento en fin d'ouvrage :
il explique la notion abordée dans l'exercice.

→ Regarder la table des matières (p. 92)
pour connaître tous les points du programme abordés dans les exercices.

→ Noter les indices sur la dernière page (p. 95) :
un par chapitre, ils prouvent que l'enquête avance et que l'histoire est bien comprise.

Coordination éditoriale : Anne-Sophie Cayrey
Corrections : Hélène Cœur
Maquette intérieure : Thierry Méléard
Composition : Compo 2000
Responsable de l'édition : Anne-Maty Niang Dagbo

1

The adventure begins

1

I am at the airport in London. One year ago* exactly, I was[1] here, at the same airport, waiting for the plane for Barbados*. This year, I'm not travelling, but I'm waiting for a very special friend. His name is Jeremy, and he is… we are…, no, it's better if I tell you the whole story. At the end, you will understand why I am here.

First, let me introduce myself. My name is Lucy and I am fourteen years old. I live in London with my parents. My father is a photographer and my mother teaches history. I go to school, of course, where my results are good, but nothing exceptional. In fact, I'm a very ordinary girl. Nothing very interesting or exciting happened in my life before last summer, when I met[21] Jeremy. This is how the story began[3].

---

one year ago : il y a un an
Barbados : la Barbade (île dans les Petites Antilles, mer des Caraïbes)

Que s'est-il passé d'extraordinaire dans la vie de Lucy ?

Pour le savoir, coche les deux bonnes réponses.
As-tu retenu ce que Lucy raconte ?

1 **a.** Lucy dit tout de suite pourquoi Jeremy est pour elle un ami particulier. . . . . ☐
b. Elle promet que tu le sauras à la fin de l'histoire. . . . ☒
2 **a.** Lucy avait déjà eu une vie passionnante avant de rencontrer Jeremy pour la première fois. . . . . ☐
b. Elle n'avait pas vécu d'aventures extraordinaires avant l'été dernier. . . . . ☒

→ LIS LE CORRIGÉ N° 1 PAGE 9.

RACONTER AU PASSÉ

Dans quelle phrase Lucy parle-t-elle au passé ?

a. I was waiting for the plane.
b. I am waiting for a special friend.

Tu as répondu a → VA VOIR LE N° 6.
Tu as répondu b → VA VOIR LE N° 5.

mémo 3

2

Tu t'es trompé(e). Il y en a 8 : went (go) - was (be) - said (say) - thought (think) - spent (spend) - saw (see) - stood (stand) - came (come). → *Lis le n° 4.*

3

Bonne réponse. → Va lire le chapitre 2.

4

'Are you all right?' I asked. It was a stupid question because it was clear that he was *not* all right.

He didn't answer, but continued looking at me, dazed* and confused*.

I looked at him again. He was a boy from the island, perhaps a little older than me, tall and slim with curly black hair.

'What's your name?' I tried again. 'Do you speak English? What happened? Why are you wet?'

I stopped. What was this? A police interrogation*?

In a soft voice, he finally spoke[32]: 'I don't know. I don't remember anything. Where am I? Who are you?'

'My name's Lucy', I said, happy to finally answer a question. 'I'm on holiday with my parents. I'm from London, in England. I was walking on the beach when I saw you. Where are you from?'

'I don't know. My head hurts*. I don't know who I am or where I'm from. Can you help me? Please?'

dazed : hébété
confused : désorienté
an interrogation : un interrogatoire
my head hurts : ma tête me fait mal

Ce garçon va-t-il réussir à dire ce qui lui est arrivé ?

« Je ne me souviens de rien » explique le garçon à Lucy. Comment le lui dit-il ?

Recopie la phrase.

I don't know who I am or where I'm from

C'est ton PREMIER INDICE.
N'oublie pas de le noter sur ta page-indices page 95.

FAIRE DES COMPARAISONS

Le garçon paraît à Lucy un peu plus âgé qu'elle.

Quel est le mot qui complète correctement cette phrase ?

Jeremy is a little older . . . than . . . Lucy.

a. than **b.** that

Tu as répondu a → VA VOIR LE N° 3.
Tu as répondu b → VA VOIR LE N° 7.

mémo I

5

Mauvaise réponse : 'I am waiting for a special friend.' *signifie « J'attends un ami particulier. » Avec* 'I am…', *Lucy parle au présent.* → *Lis maintenant le n° 6.*

6

Last August, I went[13] to the beautiful island of Barbados with my parents. A friend of my father has a villa on the beach. As she was working in New York, the house was[1] empty. It was paradise. No school, no homework (except the horrible holiday workbook my parents buy me every summer) and no rain. No friends, it's true, but you can't have everything.

I don't have any brothers or sisters, so I often do things alone. I don't mind being alone*, I imagine all sorts of adventures and mysteries. During this holiday, my father was working, so he went into the town to take photos in the street or in the market. My mother said[26] that the sun was bad for her skin*, so she stayed on the veranda, reading her book. I thought[38] that the sun was fabulous – don't forget that I live in London – and I spent[33] my time swimming in the sea. The days passed and then one day, almost* at the end of the holiday, I was walking on the beach looking for shells*. I wanted to make some bracelets for my friends in England. Suddenly, I saw[27] something strange. I thought it was some old clothes, forgotten*

I don't mind being alone : ça m'est égal d'être seule
her skin : sa peau
almost : presque
a shell : un coquillage
forgotten : oublié

by someone on the beach. Then, to my great surprise, the clothes stood[34] up and started walking towards* me! I am not afraid of many things (except snakes, but that's another story), but I admit that I was a little anxious at this moment. The 'thing' came[4] nearer* and I saw that it was a boy, a very wet boy.

Lucy va-t-elle aborder ce garçon étrange?

Pour le savoir, coche les deux bonnes réponses.
Qu'avait fait Lucy durant cet été-là ?

1 **a.** Elle avait séjourné avec ses parents dans une villa à la Barbade prêtée par une amie de son père. . . . . . . ☑
b. Elle avait séjourné à la Barbade dans une villa que possédaient là-bas ses parents. . . . . ☐
2 **a.** Elle trouva un jour sur la plage un tas de détritus. . . ☐
b. Elle vit un jour venir vers elle un garçon tout trempé. . ☑

➡ LIS LE CORRIGÉ N° 2 PAGE 9.

RACONTER AU PASSÉ

Dans ce paragraphe, Lucy emploie plusieurs verbes au prétérit simple (temps du passé). Compte-les. Combien y en a-t-il d'irréguliers ?

6 8

Si tu as répondu 6 ➡ VA VOIR LE N° 2.
Si tu as répondu 8 ➡ VA VOIR LE N° 4.

mémo 3

towards : vers
nearer : plus près

7

Tu t'es trompé(e) ! C'est than *et non* that *qui introduit ici l'autre élément de la comparaison (Lucy).* 'Jeremy is a little older than Lucy.' = *Jeremy est un peu plus âgé que Lucy.* → *Rends-toi vite au chapitre 2 !*

Corrigés des questions de compréhension

1

1. b. Elle promet que tu le sauras à la fin de l'histoire.
At the end you will understand why I am here. (tu comprendras)

2. b. Elle n'avait pas vécu d'aventures extraordinaires avant l'été dernier.
Nothing very interesting or exciting happened in my life before last summer. (Rien de très intéressant ne m'était arrivé)

2

1. a. Elle avait séjourné avec ses parents dans une villa à la Barbade prêtée par une amie de son père.
A friend of my father has a villa on the beach.

2. b. Elle vit un jour venir vers elle un garçon tout trempé.
The 'thing' came nearer and I saw that it was a boy, a very wet boy.

The lost boy

1 

'Please help me', he repeated. His large brown eyes looked at me desperately. I knew[17] I couldn't say no. This boy needed help, but first, he needed some dry clothes. I looked nervously at the house. Could I go there* with this boy? I imagined my mother's reaction. She would call* the hospital and the police, and I would never know who the boy was and where he came[4] from. No, he couldn't come with me to the house.

'Wait here', I said[26], 'next to this tree'.

I returned to the house. My mother was reading on the veranda.

'Mum, I'm going into town to buy some postcards.'

'Mmm, OK', she answered, without looking at me.

Could I go there… ? : Est-ce que je pouvais y aller… ?
she would call : elle appellerait

I took[36] a pair of shorts and a T-shirt from my father's bedroom, a bag from the kitchen for the wet clothes, and ran[25] to the tree where the boy was waiting. I politely looked in the other direction while he changed his clothes. I had[14] an idea.

'Look in your pockets', I said, 'perhaps you'll find something with your name on it.'

He put[23] his hand in the pocket of his wet clothes. There *was*[1] something there, but it wasn't a name and address; it was a key.

'What's that key?' I asked.

Où cette clé emmènera nos deux héros ?

Pour le savoir, coche les deux bonnes réponses.

Que pourrait faire Lucy pour aider ce garçon tout trempé qui a perdu la mémoire ?

1 **a.** Si elle l'emmenait dans la villa, sa mère le soignerait. ☐
b. Elle pense que le mieux est d'aller en cachette chercher des vêtements secs. ☐
2 **a.** Elle lui demande de regarder dans ses poches. . . . . ☐
b. Elle lui montre une clé tombée de sa poche.. . . . . . ☐

➡ **LIS LE CORRIGÉ N° 1 PAGE 20.**

PARLER DE POSSIBILITÉ

Lucy savait qu'elle ne « pouvait pas » dire non : 'I knew I couldn't say no.'

À quel temps est cette phrase ?

a. au présent **b.** au passé

Tu as répondu a ➡ VA VOIR LE N° 4.
Tu as répondu b ➡ VA VOIR LE N° 6.

mémo II

2

Réponse incorrecte. Avec le verbe go + in, 'Let's go in' *signifie « Entrons ».* → *Lis le n° 8.*

3

'Jack's Restaurant.' I looked at the boy. 'Do you live here? Do you work here?'
'I'm not sure', he answered. 'Yes, perhaps I live here'.
'Let's go in,' I suggested. I opened the door and we

went[13] in. I imagined a big, happy family, waiting for him behind the door. But no, the restaurant was empty. A sad old man was cleaning the tables. He looked at me and he looked at the boy, but his expression didn't change. He didn't recognize him.
'Do you want something?' he asked.
'Umm, yes.' I forgot[10] that people normally go into restaurants to* eat or drink something. 'Two orange juices, please.'
'Sorry', I said to the boy, 'do you like orange juice?' He was, after all, perfectly capable of choosing his drink, without help from me.
'Yes, very much', he answered and smiled for the second time. My heart jumped again.
We sat[30] down at the bar and drank[6] our juice.
'Do you see anything you recognize?' I asked.
The boy looked at the tables, the chairs and the sad old man.
'No, nothing. Perhaps my name is Jack, like the restaurant, but I can't see anything here that is going to help...'
He stopped and put his head in his hands. 'I can't believe it. I'm lost*... lost...'

to eat or drink : pour manger ou boire
lost : perdu

Comment ce pauvre garçon va-t-il s'en sortir ?

Pour le découvrir, coche les deux bonnes réponses.

1 Pourquoi Lucy veut-elle entrer dans le restaurant ?

a. Le garçon se demande en effet s'il habite là. . . . . . . ☒
b. Elle veut lui faire manger quelque chose. . . . . ☐

2 Pourquoi le garçon est-il soudain désemparé ?

a. La vue de ce vieil homme triste lui fait peur. . . . . . . ☐
b. Ici non plus il ne se rappelle absolument rien. . . . . . ☒

➡ **LIS LE CORRIGÉ N° 3 PAGE 20.**

FAIRE DES SUGGESTIONS

Que veut dire la phrase de Lucy : 'Let's go in' ?

a. Sortons. **b.** Entrons.

Tu as répondu a ➡ **VA VOIR LE N° 2.**
Tu as répondu b ➡ **VA VOIR LE N° 8.**

mémo 21

4

Non, cette phrase n'est pas au présent, car le prétérit knew *(du verbe* know*) du début indique déjà que la phrase est au passé.* → *Lis le n° 6.*

5

Non, le comparatif de supériorité de big *est* bigger.
→ *Lis le chapitre 3.*

6

Second stupid question of the day, I thought[38]. If he has lost* his memory, how can he recognize* the key? I took it in my hand and looked at the key ring*. It was a small anchor.

'Let's walk into the town', I suggested. 'Perhaps you will see someone or something that you remember.'

We walked on the beach in silence: the blond English girl next to the dark island boy, wearing clothes ten times too big for him.

What can you say to someone who doesn't know who he is? Who's your favourite pop star? What school do you go to? I finally thought of something. 'Does your head still hurt*?' I asked.

He looked at me, and smiled for the first time. What a difference! His face now seemed soft and kind.

'Thank you', he said, 'it hurts a little here.' He touched the back of his head. 'Can you look for me?'

'Someone or something hit[16] you', I said, examining his head.

We continued walking, but then Jeremy suddenly stopped.

if he has lost : s'il a perdu
recognize : reconnaître
a key ring : un porte-clés
Does your head still hurt? : Ta tête te fait toujours mal ?

'What is it?' I asked.

He didn't answer, but his face was distant again. He was looking, hypnotized, at the door of a restaurant.

'Are you hungry?' I said, trying to use my imagination.

'No, I'm not hungry,' he answered, *'Jack's Restaurant... Jack's restaurant...* Lucy, I think I'm beginning to remember something.'

Va-t-il retrouver aussitôt toute sa mémoire ?

Pour le savoir, coche les deux bonnes réponses.

1 Comment Lucy arrive-t-elle à faire parler ce garçon ?

a. Elle lui demande à quel collège il va. . . . . ☐
b. Elle lui demande si sa tête le fait toujours souffrir. . . ☒

2 Comment le garçon se souvient-il tout à coup de quelque chose ?

a. En voyant par hasard la façade d'un restaurant. . . . ☒
b. À cause du mystérieux porte-clés en forme d'ancre. . ☐

→ **LIS LE CORRIGÉ N° 2 PAGE 20.**

EXPRIMER LE FUTUR

Que veut dire la phrase de Lucy : 'Perhaps you will see someone or something' ?

a. Tu verras peut-être quelqu'un ou quelque chose.
b. Tu verrais peut-être quelqu'un ou quelque chose.

Tu as répondu a → VA VOIR LE N° 3.
Tu as répondu b → VA VOIR LE N° 9.

mémo 16

7

Il s'agit bien du superlatif de supériorité.

→ *Lis maintenant le chapitre 3.*

8

We finished our drinks, paid[22] the old man and left[19] the restaurant. I thought[38] again about the key

and the anchor. Where do you find anchors? I thought. On boats, of course.
'Let's try the harbour*', I suggested. 'Perhaps someone there will recognize you.'
We walked to the harbour. The boy spoke[32] again: 'When I saw[27] the name of the restaurant, I remembered two men. One of them had a gun*... I was afraid.'
'Where?' I said. 'Where were[1] you?'
But he didn't remember. We walked onto the jetty*. The yachts, floating in the transparent blue water, were beautiful. We looked at the names, *'Albatross'*, *'Ocean Wind'*, *'Pirate's Paradise'*. The boy suddenly stopped in front of one of the biggest yachts.
'Uncle Jack', he said, 'the yacht... Lucy, I know this yacht.'
'So what do we do now?' I asked. 'It was easy to go into a restaurant or a bar to see if someone knew you, but to go on someone's yacht...'
The boy took the key from his pocket and looked at the anchor. 'Here's a key', he said, 'and there's a door. Come with me.'

the harbour : le port
a gun : un pistolet
the jetty : la jetée

He leapt[18] onto the yacht and put[23] the key into the door of the cabin.

Lucy et le garçon vont-ils découvrir quelque chose sur ce bateau ?

Pour le savoir, coche la bonne réponse.

En arrivant au port, qu'est-ce qui revient alors en mémoire au garçon ?

- **a.** Deux hommes qui le menaçaient avec un couteau. ☐
- **b.** Le nom d'un des yachts amarrés le long de la jetée. ☒

→ LIS LE CORRIGÉ N° 4 PAGE 20.

Quel est le nom du bateau ?

albatross

C'est ton **DEUXIÈME INDICE.**

N'oublie pas de le noter sur ta page-indices page 95.

FAIRE DES COMPARAISONS

Dans la phrase 'The boy stopped in front of one of the biggest yachts', **à quelle forme est l'adjectif *big* ?**

- **a.** au comparatif de supériorité
- **b.** au superlatif de supériorité

Tu as répondu a → VA VOIR LE N° 5.
Tu as répondu b → VA VOIR LE N° 7.

mémo 2

9

Tu t'es trompé(e). 'Perhaps you will see someone or something.' *signifie « Tu verras peut-être quelqu'un ou quelque chose. » En utilisant le modal* will, *Lucy fait, en parlant, une sorte de pari (« peut-être bien… »).* → *Lis le n° 3.*

Corrigé des questions de compréhension

1

1. b. Elle pense que le mieux est d'aller en cachette chercher des vêtements secs.
This boy needed help, but first, he needed some dry clothes.

2. a. Elle lui demande de regarder dans ses poches.
Look in your pockets.

2

1. b. Elle lui demande si sa tête le fait toujours souffrir.
Does your head still hurt?

2. a. En voyant par hasard la façade d'un restaurant.
He was looking, hypnotized, at the door of a restaurant.

3

1. a. Le garçon se demande en effet s'il habite là.
Yes, perhaps I live here.

2. b. Ici non plus il ne se rappelle absolument rien.
Do you see anything you recognize? – No, nothing.

4

b. Le nom d'un des yachts amarrés le long de la jetée.
The boy suddenly stopped in front of one of the biggest yachts.

A mysterious boat

1 

The boy put[23] the key in the door. Slowly he turned it to the left. The door opened! He smiled at me; he had finally found* a piece of the puzzle. We went[13] down the stairs and found[9] ourselves in a lounge*. It was[1] a big yacht. There were[1] several open doors; I could see bedrooms, a kitchen and an office.

'Was this his home?' I asked myself. It seemed incredible that someone could *live* on a yacht like this.

On the table next to the sofa, there was a book. The boy opened it and looked at the front page.

'Jeremy Robinson', he said softly.

'Jeremy Robinson?' I repeated. 'Who is he? The writer?'

'No, Lucy', he answered, patiently, 'It's me.

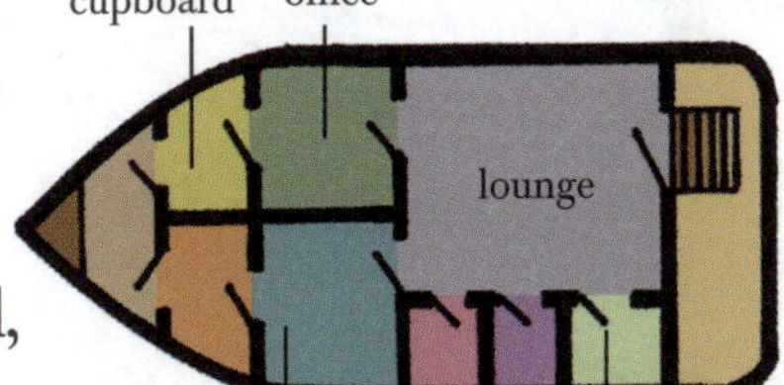

---

he had found : il avait trouvé
we found ourselves in a lounge : nous nous trouvâmes dans un salon

This is my book. It is my name.'
I smiled at him. 'Hello, Jeremy'.
Suddenly, we heard[15] a noise behind us. Someone was coming down the stairs!

Qui est cette personne qui descend les marches ?

Pour le savoir, coche la bonne réponse.
Comment Jeremy arrive-t-il, à bord du yacht, à savoir finalement qui il est ?

- **a.** Il tombe par hasard sur un livre à son nom. .... ☒
- **b.** Il aperçoit son nom sur une page d'agenda. .... ☐

➡ LIS LE CORRIGÉ N° 1 PAGE 30.

RACONTER AU PASSÉ

À quel temps est cette phrase de Lucy ?

'He had finally found a piece of the puzzle.'
a. au passé **b.** au présent

Tu as répondu a ➡ VA VOIR LE N° 5.
Tu as répondu b ➡ VA VOIR LE N° 6.

mémo 4

2

Non, ta réponse est fausse, car le pronom utilisé est you *(tu/vous). → Lis le n° 3.*

3

Jeremy took[36] my hand and together we ran[25] to the park. He changed his clothes behind a tree.

Then he began[3] to tell me…

'When I first saw[27] my name in the book and then when I spoke to my uncle', he explained, 'my memory came back.'

'But why do you live with your uncle?' I asked. 'Where are your parents?'

His face became[2] serious and sad. 'Let's sit down here. Let me explain', he said, pointing to a bench*.

'Lucy, my parents died last Christmas in a car accident. I went to live with Uncle Jack on his yacht. It seemed to be a fabulous life, travelling from island to island, from continent to continent.'

'How do you go to school?' I interrupted.

'I don't', said Jeremy.

'Life without school! What a fabulous idea!'

'But I still have to do my schoolwork. Believe me* Lucy, it's not fun. I don't have any friends of my age or anyone who can help me when I have a problem.'

'I suppose you're right', I admitted, 'Sorry, I interrupted your story…'

Jeremy continued: 'After a few months, things

a bench : un banc
believe me : crois-moi

began to seem* strange. What is my uncle's job? Where does his money come from? On the yacht, there are some rooms which are always locked* and my uncle says that I must never, never try to go in. He seems a nice man, and I think he *is* a nice man, but I also think that he's doing something bad.'

Oncle Jack aurait-il une vie cachée ?

Pour le savoir, coche les deux bonnes réponses.
Que nous apprend Jeremy sur sa vie ?

1 a. Il était parti sur le yacht avec son oncle parce qu'il aimait voyager. .... ☐
b. Son oncle l'avait recueilli sur son yacht à la mort de ses parents. .... ☒
2 a. Il regrette de ne pas pouvoir aller à l'école. .... ☒
b. Il trouve que son oncle est un homme méchant. . . . ☐

→ **LIS LE CORRIGÉ N° 3 PAGE 30.**

PARLER D'OBLIGATION

'I still have to do my schoolwork' explique Jeremy à Lucy.
Que veut-il dire par là ?

a. Il doit faire des devoirs comme n'importe quel élève.
b. Il doit faire des devoirs parce que quelqu'un l'exige.

Tu as répondu a → VA VOIR LE N° 9.
Tu as répondu b → VA VOIR LE N° 8.

mémo 17

seem : sembler
locked : fermé à clé

4

Mauvaise réponse ! À la différence du français, les adverbes de fréquence se placent en anglais avant le verbe, sauf avec le verbe be ! → *Va au chapitre 4.*

5

Behind us, a man came[4] into the room. He was tall, with silver grey hair. He was wearing blue trousers and a yellow and red shirt.

'Uncle Jack! You're Uncle Jack, of course!' said Jeremy.

'Jeremy!' exclaimed the man. 'What happened? I was very worried. Where did you go last night, after... after... you know...?'

He stopped and looked at me nervously. 'We can talk about that later.'

I felt[8] very uneasy*. I looked at Jeremy. He had[14] a strange expression on his face.

Uncle Jack spoke[32] again : 'I'm going to phone the coastguard* to tell them that you're all right. Why are you wearing those strange clothes? Would you and your... um, friend like something to drink? Where's my phone...?' He went into the office.

---

uneasy : mal à l'aise
the coastguard : la gendarmerie maritime

Jeremy went into one of the bedrooms and came out with some of his clothes.
'Quick,' he said, 'let's go.'
'What?' I exclaimed. 'But why?'
I couldn't believe it*. For the first time in my life, I was on a millionaire's yacht, and my friend wanted to leave!

Mais pourquoi Jeremy veut-il aussitôt descendre du bateau ?

Pour le savoir, coche les deux bonnes réponses.
Comment l'oncle Jack réagit-il en découvrant Jeremy et Lucy ?

1 a. Il se montre très aimable avec Lucy. . . . . ☐
b. Il est visiblement gêné de parler devant elle. . . . . ☐
2 a. Il est soulagé de retrouver Jeremy. . . . . ☐
b. Il ne tient pas à appeler la gendarmerie. . . . . ☐

➡ LIS LE CORRIGÉ N° 2 PAGE 30.

EXPRIMER UN DÉSIR

Dans la question 'Would you like something to drink?', **que demande l'oncle ?**

a. Aimerait-elle boire quelque chose ?
b. Aimerais-tu boire quelque chose ?

Tu as répondu a ➡ VA VOIR LE N° 2.
Tu as répondu b ➡ VA VOIR LE N° 3.

mémo 10

I couldn't believe it : je n'en revenais pas

6

Non, la phrase est au passé, comme l'indique la forme prétérit had *suivie du participe passé (=plus-que-parfait)* → *Va au n° 5.*

7

Réponse correcte. → *Va maintenant au chapitre 4.*

8

Tu t'es trompé(e). L'emploi de have to *(+ base verbale) exprime une obligation due simplement aux circonstances. (Il faut quand même qu'il fasse des devoirs comme n'importe quel élève.)* → *Lis le n° 9.*

9

'But why did you suddenly want to leave[19] the yacht?' I asked.

'Because I remembered last night,' he replied. 'We were sailing* not very far from the harbour. My uncle often leaves[19] me alone on deck* if he is working in his office or if he is talking to friends. It's a big yacht, but when it's not windy, it's relatively easy to sail.'

---

sail : ici, manœuvrer
the deck : le pont

He seemed so cool; I tried to imagine myself, alone, sailing that enormous yacht on the ocean… Jeremy continued: 'Then I saw that there was a problem with the boom*. I tried to fix it, but I couldn't do it alone. I went down to the office to ask for my uncle's help. The door was open and I saw a laptop*.'

Jeremy's eyes were closed. All the memories were coming back.

'When I entered the office, I looked at the computer. On the screen I read[24] the words "Operation Blue Lagoon". There was a list of names, and pictures… pictures of animals. No, they were reptiles', he paused, '… snakes and tortoises. Then I saw my uncle in the back of the room. Next to him, there was a man. He was holding* a gun to my uncle's

the boom : la bôme (pièce de bois horizontale sur laquelle est fixée la voile)
a laptop : un ordinateur portable
hold : tenir

head. I was afraid and tried to leave silently. But the man heard me and started running towards me with the gun. I panicked and ran up the stairs to the deck. Then something – the boom, I suppose – hit[16] me on the head, and I fell[7] into the sea…'

Qui est donc ce personnage menaçant ?

Pour le savoir, coche les deux bonnes réponses.
Qu'était-il arrivé à Jeremy la veille ?

1 **a.** Il avait joué sur l'ordinateur. . . . . [ ]
b. Il avait essayé d'arranger la bôme. . . . . [x]
2 **a.** Jeremy plongea dans la mer. . . . . [ ]
b. Quelque chose le fit tomber à l'eau. . . . . [x]

➡ **LIS LE CORRIGÉ N° 4 PAGE 30.**

Quels mots Jeremy a-t-il eu le temps de lire sur l'écran de l'ordinateur ?

Operation Blue Lagoon

C'est ton TROISIÈME INDICE.
N'oublie pas de le noter sur ta page-indices page 95.

PARLER DE FRÉQUENCE

Dans la phrase 'My uncle often leaves me alone', **où est placé l'adverbe** 'often' **?**

a. après le verbe   **b.** avant le verbe

Tu as répondu a ➡ **VA VOIR LE N° 4.**
Tu as répondu b ➡ **VA VOIR LE N° 7.**

mémo 6

Corrigé des questions de compréhension

1

1. a. Il tombe par hasard sur un livre à son nom.
On the table (...) there was a book. The boy opened it and looked at the front page. 'Jeremy Robinson' he said (...) 'It's me. This is my book. It is my name.'

2

1. b. Il est visiblement gêné de parler devant elle.
He stopped and looked at me nervously. 'We can talk about that later.' (Nous pouvons parler de ça plus tard.)

2. a. Il est soulagé de retrouver Jeremy.
I was very worried. (J'étais très inquiet.)

3

1. b. Son oncle l'avait recueilli sur son yacht à la mort de ses parents.
My parents died (...) in a car accident. I went to live with Uncle Jack.

2. a. Il regrette de ne pas pouvoir aller à l'école.
Believe me Lucy, it's not fun. I don't have any friends of my age.

4

1. b. Il avait essayé d'arranger la bôme.
There was a problem with the boom. I tried to fix it.

2. b. Quelque chose le fit tomber à l'eau.
Something (...) hit me on the head, and I fell into the sea.

4 Midnight at the harbour

1

'Then I swam[35] and I swam,' continued Jeremy, 'until I finally reached* the beach. There, I collapsed*.'

'What a story!' I thought[38]. Then I asked : 'Why do you think the man had a gun? And why did he run towards you with the gun?'

'He probably thought that I read[24] all the information on the computer screen, but I didn't read it because I didn't have the time. As* I said, I only saw[27] the words "Operation Blue Lagoon", pictures of reptiles and a list of names.'

---

until I reached : jusqu'à ce que j'atteigne
collapse : s'effondrer
as I said : comme j'ai dit

'What do we do now?' I asked. I don't know why I said 'we'. Now that he could remember who he was and where he lived, Jeremy didn't need* me. He read my thoughts*: 'Lucy, you helped me to find the yacht. I can't do the rest alone. We must find the information on the computer, print it and take it to the police. I'm sure it's something bad.'

'But your Uncle Jack…' I protested.

'I know, I know… Is he a criminal? I don't know, he's always kind to me. I think he is in more danger from those men than from the police. If the police catch them, it could save my uncle.'

I looked at the beautiful harbour. Police? Criminals? Guns? What sort of holiday was this?

need : avoir besoin de
my thoughts : mes pensées

Quel va être le plan de Jeremy pour s'emparer de ces documents compromettants ?

Pour le savoir, coche les deux bonnes réponses.

1 Pourquoi l'homme au pistolet avait-il poursuivi Jeremy ?

a. Jeremy avait noté toutes les informations affichées sur l'écran de l'ordinateur. . . . . ☒
b. L'homme avait cru que Jeremy les avait lues. . . . . . . ☒

2 Que dit Jeremy de son oncle ?

a. Il est toujours gentil avec lui.. ☒
b. Il ne court aucun danger.. . . . . ☐

➡ LIS LE CORRIGÉ N° 1 PAGE 42.

PARLER DE POSSIBILITÉ

Quelle est la bonne traduction des mots soulignés dans la phrase de Jeremy ?

'If the police catch those men, it could save my uncle.'
a. Cela pouvait sauver mon oncle.
b. Cela pourrait sauver mon oncle.

Tu as répondu a ➡ **VA VOIR LE N° 5.**
Tu as répondu b ➡ **VA VOIR LE N° 7.**

mémo 12

2

Faux ! Le prétérit (went) *dans la subordonnée de condition* 'If I went out…' *(si je sortais) montre que l'on est dans l'irréel. La principale exprime donc le conditionnel :* 'my parents would wake up.' *(mes parents se réveilleraient.)* → *Lis le n° 9.*

3

Non, Lucy s'exprime ici au futur. 'I'll write them later.' =*Je les écrirai plus tard.* → *Lis le n° 4.*

4

If I went out of the front door, my parents would probably wake up. I remembered that a light was automatically activated when there was a movement near the front door. That could easily wake up my parents! There was one other solution. I looked out of the window. Five metres? Six? No, I wasn't going to jump, but I remembered something from the adventure books I read when I was younger. If children needed to escape from their bedrooms, they always knotted together the sheets* from their bed. So that is exactly what I did[5]. Five minutes later, my feet touched the ground. Twenty minutes later, I was with Jeremy at the harbour.
'Are you ready?' he asked.
'Yes, let's go', I answered, hoping to give the impression that I did this sort of thing every night. We silently went down the stairs of the boat and opened the door with Jeremy's key. He switched on a table lamp. Then we crossed the lounge and tried

knot the sheets : nouer les draps

to open the door to the office. It was locked, and this time Jeremy didn't have the key!

Lucy et Jeremy vont-ils réussir à parvenir jusqu'à l'ordinateur ?

Pour le découvrir, coche les deux bonnes réponses.

1 Comment Lucy a-t-elle pu sortir sans réveiller ses parents ?

a. Elle a pu facilement passer par la porte d'entrée. . . . ☐
b. Elle a trouvé le moyen de descendre par la fenêtre. . ☒

2 Que se passa-t-il quand Lucy et Jeremy se retrouvèrent au bateau ?

a. Ils eurent des problèmes pour pénétrer dans le yacht. ☐
b. Ils ne purent pas entrer dans le bureau. . . . . ☒

➡ LIS LE CORRIGÉ N° 3 PAGE 42.

EXPRIMER LE CONDITIONNEL

Quelle est la bonne traduction de la phrase : 'If I went out of the front door, my parents would wake up' ?

a. Si je sors par la porte d'entrée, mes parents se réveilleront.
b. Si je sortais par la porte d'entrée, mes parents se réveilleraient.

Tu as répondu a ➡ VA VOIR LE N° 2.
Tu as répondu b ➡ VA VOIR LE N° 9.

mémo 9

5

Faux. Jeremy fait ici une supposition : si on les attrape, son oncle « serait peut-être » sauvé. If the police catch those men, it could save my uncle.' = *Cela pourrait sauver mon oncle.* → *Lis le n° 7.*

6

Oui, il s'agit bien, avec l'emploi de have to, *d'une obligation due aux circonstances.* → *Va au chapitre 5.*

7

'It's too risky to go back to the yacht now', said Jeremy. 'I'll have to answer* too many questions. Let's go back tonight when my uncle is sleeping. Why don't we meet[21] at the harbour at midnight? My uncle normally goes to bed early.'

'At the harbour at midnight', I repeated. 'But where are you going before?'

'I'll stay here for the moment', he answered, 'then I know a café where I can wait.'

I walked back to the villa. My mother was still reading on the veranda and my father was looking at some photos that he wanted to send to a magazine in London.

'Lucy!' they exclaimed, 'we had lunch without you. Where were you?'

I'll have to answer : il faudra que je réponde

'Sorry', I answered, 'I didn't see the time.'

'Did you buy the postcards?' asked my mother.

Postcards? What was she talking about? Oh yes, the postcards for my friends!

'Um... yes!' I answered, a little too enthusiastically. 'They're in my bag. I'll write them later.' I knew[17] she would forget.

The rest of the afternoon passed slowly. I took[36] my magazine and joined my mother on the veranda. We chatted about fashion, cinema and our friends in London. All the time I was watching the clock in the kitchen; five o'clock, six o'clock... the hours were passing so slowly!

Finally, at half past ten, we all went[13] to bed. I waited in my bedroom... eleven o'clock, half past eleven. It was time to go... but how?

Comment Lucy va-t-elle sortir de chez elle ?

Pour le savoir, coche les deux bonnes réponses.

1 Pourquoi Lucy et Jeremy se séparent-ils ?

a. Jeremy préfère qu'ils se retrouvent, pour aller sur le yacht, le matin suivant. .... ☐

b. Jeremy préfère qu'ils retournent au yacht quand son oncle sera couché. .... ☑

2 Que vient faire ici cette histoire de cartes postales ?

a. Lucy avait dit à sa mère qu'elle sortait pour en acheter. ☑

b. Sa mère lui avait demandé d'en acheter pour elle... ☐

➡ LIS LE CORRIGÉ N° 2 PAGE 42.

EXPRIMER LE FUTUR

Quelle est la bonne traduction de cette phrase de Lucy à sa mère : 'I'll write them later.' ?

a. Je les écrirais plus tard. **b.** Je les écrirai plus tard.

Tu as répondu a ➡ VA VOIR LE N° 3.
Tu as répondu b ➡ VA VOIR LE N° 4.

mémo 16

8

Tu t'es trompé(e). L'emploi de have to *montre qu'il s'agit d'une obligation due aux circonstances (Tu veux dire qu'il faut qu'on entre...)* → *Va au chapitre 5.*

9

'I know where the key is', whispered* Jeremy

whisper : chuchoter

'but it's on Jack's key ring. He normally puts it on the table next to his bed.'

'Are you saying that we have to go into his bedroom?' I whispered.

'Yes', answered Jeremy 'it's this door here. Listen, he's snoring*.'

Together we stood[34] in front of the bedroom door. Very slowly and quietly, Jeremy opened it. The light from the lamp in the lounge shone[28] into the bedroom; we could see the keys on the table. Jeremy took them but they made[20] a noise.

The snoring stopped. My heart was beating so fast and loudly* that I thought[38] that Jack would hear it and wake up. But no, he changed position without opening his eyes... and started snoring again. Jeremy had the keys and we shut[29] the door silently.

In the office we switched on the computer.

'Oh, no!' exclaimed Jeremy, 'why didn't I think of that?'

I looked at the screen and saw 'PASSWORD?'

'Try "Jack",' I suggested.

'J-A-C-K', typed Jeremy. No, it wasn't that.

---

snore : ronfler
loudly : bruyamment

'Try the name of his wife, of his children or of his… dog.' I continued.

'No wife, no children… and certainly no dog,' answered Jeremy. He thought for a moment and said[26], 'Perhaps…'

He typed something. 'PASSWORD ACCEPTED'.

'Excellent', I smiled enthusiastically, 'You're the best! What did you write?'

His face became[2] serious. 'I typed "P-E-T-E-R",' he said, 'it was my father's name.'

I started to say that I was sorry, but we were suddenly interrupted by *Like a Virgin* by Madonna. Uncle Jack's mobile phone was ringing... and it was in the office, next to the computer!

Jack va-t-il se réveiller ?

Pour le savoir, coche la bonne réponse.
Pourquoi la clé du bureau leur pose-t-elle un problème ?

- **a.** Jeremy ne sait pas où la chercher. . . . . ☐
- **b.** Ils risquent de réveiller l'oncle en la prenant. . . . . . . ☒

➡ LIS LE CORRIGÉ N° 4 PAGE 42.

Quels mots utilise Lucy pour dire : « Nous allumâmes l'ordinateur » ?

We switched on the computer

C'est ton QUATRIÈME INDICE.
N'oublie pas de le noter sur ta page-indices page 95.

PARLER D'OBLIGATION

Quelle sorte d'obligation Lucy exprime-t-elle dans sa question ?

'Are you saying that *we have to go* into his bedroom?'

- **a.** une obligation due aux circonstances
- **b.** une obligation voulue par quelqu'un

Tu as répondu a ➡ VA VOIR LE N° 6.
Tu as répondu b ➡ VA VOIR LE N° 8.

mémo 17

Corrigé des questions de compréhension

1

1. b. L'homme avait cru que Jeremy les avait lues.
He probably thought that I read all the information on the computer screen.

2. a. Il est toujours gentil avec lui.
He's always kind to me.

2

1. b. Jeremy préfère qu'ils retournent au yacht quand son oncle sera couché.
Let's go back tonight when my uncle is sleeping.

2. a. Lucy avait dit à sa mère qu'elle sortait pour en acheter.
Oh yes, the postcards for my friends!

3

1. b. Elle a trouvé le moyen de descendre par la fenêtre.
If children needed to escape from their bedrooms, they always knotted together the sheets from their bed.

2. b. Ils ne purent pas entrer dans le bureau à l'intérieur du salon.
It was locked, and this time Jeremy didn't have the key!

4

b. Ils risquent de réveiller l'oncle en la prenant.
Jeremy took them but they made a noise. The snoring stopped.

5

Operation Blue Lagoon

1

'What do we do?' I whispered. 'Your uncle will see that his keys are not on his table.'

We heard[15] a noise from Jack's bedroom, he was coming! Jeremy quickly took[36] the telephone and put[23] it on the table in the lounge. He came[4] back into the office, switched off the light and closed the door. We heard Jack come into the lounge and switch on the lamp. His footsteps* became[2] louder and nearer*! Then, just before the door, he hesitated, gave[12] a 'hum!', and changed direction. Jeremy and I breathed* once again.

We heard Uncle Jack speaking on the phone.

---

his footsteps : ses pas
nearer : plus près
breathe : respirer

'I don't think he saw[27] anything... He was with a girl... No, I have no idea who she is... But I can't do that, he's my brother's son!'

Before Jack finished his conversation, we heard another noise. There was a second person in the lounge!

'Jack, who are you talking to?' said the new voice. The accent was strange: South American, I thought[38].

'To our friend...' answered Jack.

'We have to hide', whispered Jeremy. 'Quick, in that cupboard* there! I'm just going to switch off the computer.'

I opened the cupboard door and went[13] in... at precisely the moment that the office door opened.

a cupboard : un placard

Lucy a le temps de se cacher, mais que va-t-il arriver à Jeremy ?

Pour le savoir, coche les deux bonnes réponses.

1 Quel fut le bon réflexe de Jeremy en cet instant critique ?

a. Il décrocha le téléphone, mais sans répondre. . . . . . ☐
b. Il courut mettre le téléphone mobile dans le salon. ☒

2 Pourquoi la situation se complique-t-elle ?

a. Ils entendent l'oncle ouvrir la porte du bureau. . . . ☐
b. Ils entendent une autre personne entrer dans le salon. ☒

➡ LIS LE CORRIGÉ N° 1 PAGE 53.

EXPRIMER LE FUTUR

Que veut dire la phrase de Jeremy 'I'm going to switch off the computer' **?**

a. Je suis en train d'éteindre l'ordinateur.
b. Je vais éteindre l'ordinateur.

Tu as répondu a ➡ **VA VOIR LE N° 5.**
Tu as répondu b ➡ **VA VOIR LE N° 7.**

mémo 16

2

Tu t'es trompé(e). 'You're shaking' = *Tu trembles. En employant* be *au présent suivi du verbe avec* -ing, *Jeremy décrit ici Lucy « en train de trembler ».* → *Lis le n° 9.*

3

Mauvaise réponse ! 'I have to' *exprime une obligation*

au présent. 'I had to think of something different.' = *Il fallait que je pense à autre chose.* → *Lis le n° 4.*

4 

'Ha! Ha! You're not going anywhere now', I heard from outside.

The office door closed. I heard the key turn in the door, and then silence.

I waited for five minutes. They were the longest five minutes of my life. Then I opened the door. Poor Jeremy! He could not move. The sticky tape was covering his mouth and his hands were behind his back. The man was right: Jeremy was not going anywhere.

I freed* his hands and then helped him to do the rest.

'Are you all right?' asked Jeremy, 'You're shaking*.'

'Look in the cupboard', I said.

When Jeremy saw the snakes, he exclaimed 'Now, I understand. *This is* Operation Blue Lagoon! My uncle helps reptile smugglers*! But Lucy, why are you still shaking?'

---

free (verbe) : libérer
shake : trembler
a smuggler : un contrebandier

'I am only afraid of one thing', I replied, 'Snakes.'
He put his arms around me. I blushed*.
'Stop shaking', he said, 'it's finished. Now we have to escape from this yacht!'
'That's easy', I answered.
Jeremy looked at me, astonished*. 'But we can't!'

Comment Lucy et Jeremy parviendront-ils à s'échapper ?

Pour le savoir, coche les deux bonnes réponses.

1 Terrorisée au fond de son placard, que va faire Lucy ?

a. Elle attend un moment avant de sortir. . . . . ☒
b. Elle préfère sortir tout de suite. . . . . ☒ F

2 Que vient de comprendre Jeremy ?

a. L'oncle Jack est un collectionneur de reptiles. . . . . ☐
b. Il fait de la contrebande de reptiles. . . . . ☒

➡ LIS LE CORRIGÉ N° 3 PAGE 53.

ARRÊTER DE FAIRE QUELQUE CHOSE

Dans quelle phrase Jeremy dit-il à Lucy d'arrêter de trembler ?

a. You're shaking. **b.** Stop shaking.

Tu as répondu a ➡ VA VOIR LE N° 2.
Tu as répondu b ➡ VA VOIR LE N° 9.

mémo 8

I blushed : je rougis
astonished : très surpris

5

Mauvaise réponse. « Je suis en train d'éteindre… » se traduirait alors par 'I'm switching off…' *Avec* be going to, *Jeremy annonce à Lucy une décision qu'il a déjà prise.* 'I'm going to switch off…' = *Je vais éteindre…* → *Lis le n° 7.*

6

Faux. La forme interro-négative 'didn't you know' *(ne le savais-tu pas ?) exprime l'étonnement. Revois le mémo 5.* → *Va maintenant au chapitre 6.*

7

The smell* in the cupboard was horrible. Did Uncle Jack put his old socks here? I tried to breathe through* my mouth.

'Hey, Jack, look at this!' I heard the sarcastic Spanish voice. 'Little Jeremy came to see us… and now he's playing a computer game! Sorry, Jeremy, this computer is not for you, I'm going to take it with me.' His voice suddenly became angry. 'Jack, why did you give him the key?' I heard protests of innocence coming from the lounge.

the smell : l'odeur
through : à travers

'Jeremy', the man continued in the same sarcastic tone, 'your uncle and I are going for a walk. You are going to sit down here and wait for us. Your little games are finished!'

I heard the sound of sticky tape*, lots of sticky tape. The smell in the cupboard was terrible. I remembered that my mobile phone had a little lamp. Very, very quietly, I took my phone from my pocket. I switched on the lamp and looked around... I was petrified. It wasn't possible, this simply *wasn't possible.* I wanted to scream, but when I opened my mouth, nothing came out. In the cupboard, in cages, one on top of the other, there were snakes. Snakes! The only thing I am afraid of! I couldn't breathe. I closed my eyes: I had to think of something different; the sea, a chocolate cake... postcards of Barbados...

sticky tape : ruban adhésif

Lucy va-t-elle réussir à surmonter sa peur ?

Pour le découvrir, coche les deux bonnes réponses.

1 Pourquoi Lucy a-t-elle des raisons de s'inquiéter au sujet de Jeremy ?

a. Lucy entend un bruit de ruban adhésif qu'on déchire. ☒
b. Elle entend un cliquetis de chaînes. . . . . ☒

2 Quel adjectif décrit le mieux l'état de Lucy quand elle voit les serpents ?

a. afraid ☐ **b.** petrified ☒

➡ LIS LE CORRIGÉ N° 2 PAGE 53.

PARLER D'OBLIGATION

Lucy se dit qu'il lui « fallait » absolument penser à autre chose.

Quels mots emploie-t-elle pour dire cela ?

a. I have to think of something different.
b. I had to think of something different.

Tu as répondu a ➡ VA VOIR LE N° 3.
Tu as répondu b ➡ VA VOIR LE N° 4.

mémo 18

8

Bravo ! Tu peux maintenant aller au chapitre 6.

9

Jeremy continued: 'They locked the door, Lucy, didn't you know?'

'Yes', I answered. 'But let me look… Yes! We're

lucky: they left[19] the key in the door. Didn't you read adventure books when you were young?'

'Umm... yes', he said, 'but perhaps not the same books as* you...'

For the second time that night, I remembered those books.

'I need a newspaper and a hairclip*', I said.

'Here's an old newspaper', Jeremy said, 'but my lipstick and my hairclips are in my bedroom...'

I smiled. 'Very funny... I have one here, in my hair.'

I opened the newspaper and slid[31] it under the door. I pushed the key with the hairclip. The keys fell[7] onto the newspaper. I slowly slid the newspaper and the keys towards* me.

the same... as : les mêmes que
a hairclip : une barrette
towards : vers

'The keys', I announced, triumphantly.

Jeremy looked at me in astonishment. 'You're a real James Bond girl!' he exclaimed. 'Let's go!'

Où Lucy et Jeremy vont-ils maintenant aller ?

Pour le savoir, coche la bonne réponse.

Quel moyen ingénieux Lucy trouve-t-elle pour attraper la clé de l'autre côté de la serrure ?

- **a.** Elle pousse d'abord la clé avec la barrette. . . . . ☐
- **b.** Elle glisse d'abord un journal sous la porte. . . . . ☒

→ LIS LE CORRIGÉ DU N° 4 PAGE 53.

Que dit Jeremy quand il qualifie Lucy de grande aventurière ? Recopie la phrase.

You're a real James Bond Girl.

C'est ton CINQUIÈME INDICE.
N'oublie pas de le noter sur ta page-indices page 95.

EXPRIMER L'ÉTONNEMENT

Quelle est la bonne traduction des mots soulignés dans la phrase de Jeremy ?

'They locked the door, Lucy, didn't you know?'

a. le savais-tu ? **b.** ne le savais-tu pas ?

Tu as répondu a → VA VOIR LE N° 6.
Tu as répondu b → VA VOIR LE N° 8.

mémo 5

Corrigé des questions de compréhension

1

1. b. Il courut mettre le téléphone mobile dans le salon.
Jeremy quickly took the telephone and put it on the table in the lounge.

2. b. Ils entendent une autre personne entrer dans le salon.
...we heard another noise. There was a second person in the lounge!

2

1. a. Lucy entend un bruit de ruban adhésif qu'on déchire.
I heard the sound of sticky tape, lots of sticky tape.

2. b. petrified

3

1. a. Elle attend un moment avant de sortir.
I waited for five minutes. (...) Then, I opened the door.

2. b. L'oncle Jack fait de la contrebande de reptiles.
My uncle helps reptile smugglers!

4

b. Elle glisse d'abord un journal sous la porte.
I opened the newspaper and slid it under the door.

6

A surprise visit

1 

We left[19] the yacht and started walking along the beach to the villa.

'What exactly are reptile smugglers?' I asked. 'And why do they do it?'

'Reptile smugglers capture or buy reptiles in one country and transport them to another country', explained Jeremy. 'And the answer to your second question is simple. They do it for the money, a lot of money.'

'People pay money for snakes!' I exclaimed. 'For a cat, a dog or a horse, I could understand it. But for a snake…!'

'Absolutely', continued Jeremy, 'and not only for snakes. I saw[27] a programme on television; people also take tortoises and iguanas from Barbados and sell them in the United States for thousands of dollars'.

'Wow!' I said, astonished.

Then I looked at my watch. It was half past two.

'It's late now', I said, 'Why don't we sleep? Tomorrow we'll try to find the man with the computer and go to see the police.'

'You're right', answered Jeremy, 'I'm tired, too.'

We arrived in front of the villa. I had a dilemma: I didn't want to ask Jeremy to sleep another night on the beach, but I couldn't invite him into the house at 3 o'clock in the morning.

I had an idea. 'The garage is empty', I said, 'you could sleep there. I'll throw* you a pillow* and some blankets* from my bedroom window.'

'Thank you', he answered, smiling. 'A five-star garage, perfect!'

throw : lancer
a pillow : un oreiller
a blanket : une couverture

He looked up at my bedroom window and saw the sheets.

'You really are a Bond girl', he said, laughing softly.

I climbed*, not very elegantly, to my bedroom and found[9] pillows and blankets for Jeremy.

'Good night', I whispered. 'Sleep well!'

Tomorrow was going to be a difficult day…

Que va-t-il se passer le lendemain ?

Pour le savoir, coche les deux bonnes réponses.

1 Qu'est-ce qui étonne Lucy dans ce que lui apprend Jeremy?

- **a.** Que l'on puisse dépenser de l'argent pour un serpent. ☐
- **b.** Que l'on ait à en dépenser pour un chat ou un chien. ☐

2 Où Jeremy va-t-il finalement passer la nuit ?

- **a.** Dans le garage de la villa. . . . . ☐
- **b.** Dans un hôtel cinq étoiles. ☐

→ **LIS LE CORRIGÉ N° 1 PAGE 64.**

FAIRE DES SUGGESTIONS

Quelle est la bonne traduction de cette phrase ?
'You could sleep there.'

a. Tu pourrais dormir là. **b.** Tu pouvais dormir là.

Tu as répondu a → VA VOIR LE N° 5.
Tu as répondu b → VA VOIR LE N° 6.

mémo 21

climb : grimper

2

Tu t'es trompé(e). 'He mustn't see me.' = *Il ne faut pas qu'il me voie. Cette traduction montre mieux la peur que ressent Lucy.* → *Lis maintenant le n° 3.*

3

'Where's Dad?' I asked, 'I don't think he would like strange men* in the house.'

'Oh, Lucy', said my mother, laughing, 'don't worry. He was charming. I'm sure that your father would think the same thing!'

I changed the subject. 'I'm going to get some orange juice', I said, and went into the kitchen. I was afraid and wanted to talk to Jeremy.

I quietly opened the door from the kitchen into the garage. I switched on the light. The garage was empty! I went back into the kitchen and took[36] my juice. I was confused*. Where was Jeremy?

Did the man take him? Was he afraid that my parents would find him? There was also one possibility that I didn't want to consider: perhaps he thought that it was too dangerous for me and he wanted to continue alone.

---

strange men : des inconnus
confused : désorientée

Jeremy va-t-il continuer sans Lucy ?

Pour le savoir, coche les deux bonnes réponses.

Qu'est-ce qui inquiète tant Lucy ?

1 a. Sa mère a l'air de se méfier de cet inconnu. . . . . . . ☐
b. Elle pense que son père n'apprécierait pas d'avoir des inconnus chez lui. . . . . ☐
2 a. Elle ne retrouve pas Jeremy dans le garage.. . . . . . . ☐
b. Elle a peur que ses parents ne tombent sur lui. . . . . ☐

→ LIS LE CORRIGÉ N° 3 PAGE 64.

EXPRIMER LE CONDITIONNEL

Dans ces phrases, l'auxiliaire modal est souligné.

Lequel des deux permet de parler au conditionnel ?

a. I'm sure that your father would think the same thing.
b. I'm sure that your father will think the same thing.

Tu as répondu a → VA VOIR LE N° 9.
Tu as répondu b → VA VOIR LE N° 8.

mémo 9

4

Faux. 'You're very pale' *décrit un état tandis que* might *permet de dire quelque chose dont on n'est pas sûr.* 'I think you might be ill' = *Je crois que tu es peut-être malade.* → *Va maintenant au chapitre 7.*

5

The next day, I woke[40] up and heard[15] voices in the garden. I looked out of the window and I saw my mother talking to a man. They were laughing together. I didn't know the man. I didn't think my mother knew[17] anyone on the island. He then asked my mother a question and it was at that moment that my heart stopped. I recognized that voice, that South American accent! I threw[39] myself on the floor. He mustn't see me! What was he doing here? How did he know I lived here? What was he saying to my mother? Could Jeremy hear the voice from the garage? All these questions in my head… I waited in my bedroom. The voices finally stopped and I could see my mother alone again, reading her book on the veranda. Nervously, I went downstairs.

'Lucy!' exclaimed my mother. 'Are you ill? It's 12 o'clock!'

12 o'clock! Help! What could I say?

'I… um… had a bad night', I said. 'I had bad dreams and couldn't sleep. Who were you talking to?'

'Oh, I don't know his name', she answered. 'He said that he wanted to buy a villa on this beach. He asked me if I wanted to sell the house. Of course, I told[37] him that it wasn't *our* villa, but he was very charming… yes, very charming… He wanted… to visit the house, but I had to say no. I think he'll come back later.'

'Please, no, don't come back!' I thought[38]!

Cet homme reviendra-t-il rôder près de la maison ?

Pour le savoir, coche les deux bonnes réponses.

1 Est-ce que Lucy reconnaît l'homme qui parle à sa mère ?

a. Lucy reconnaît tout de suite son visage. . . . . ☐
b. Elle reconnaît son accent. ☐

2 Pourquoi la mère de Lucy parlait-elle avec cet homme ?

a. Elle lui avait fait visiter la maison. . . . . ☐
b. Elle l'avait trouvé très agréable. . . . . ☐

→ Lis le corrigé n° 2 page 64.

PARLER D'OBLIGATION

'He mustn't see me', se dit Lucy.

Quelle est la meilleure traduction de cette phrase?

a. Il ne doit pas me voir.
b. Il ne faut pas qu'il me voie.

Tu as répondu a → Va voir le n° 2.
Tu as répondu b → Va voir le n° 3.

mémo 17

6

Faux. 'You could sleep there.' = *Tu pourrais dormir là. Avec* could, *Lucy n'exprime pas ici une possibilité au passé, mais une suggestion.* → *Lis le n° 5.*

7

Bravo ! Va maintenant au chapitre 7.

8

Mauvaise réponse. Le modal will *exprime ici le futur. Revois le mémo 16.* 'I'm sure that your father would think the same thing'. = *Je suis sûre que ton père penserait la même chose.* → *Lis le n° 9.*

9

I had lunch with my mother.
'Lucy, darling', she said, 'I think you might be ill. You're not eating anything and you're very pale.'
'I'm okay, Mum', I said. 'I just have a headache*. It may be the heat*. I think I'll lie down* in my bedroom this afternoon.'
'Good idea', she answered. 'If you need anything...'

a headache : mal à la tête
it may be the heat : c'est peut-être la chaleur
lie down : s'allonger

I went[13] to my bedroom and thought[38] about the last twenty-four hours. I was sure now that Jeremy didn't want to continue without me. Perhaps he was in danger… perhaps he needed me. I got[11] up, left the house and walked towards the harbour. To my surprise, the yacht was not there. I imagined that Jeremy was a prisoner and that the smugglers were sailing for another country. Was it all my fault because I put Jeremy in the garage? I felt[8] terrible and started to cry. Slowly, I walked back along the beach. I was passing Jack's Restaurant, when something hit[16] me on the leg. I stopped. Was it my imagination? Then something hit me on the back, and again on the leg. Someone was throwing little stones at me!

Qui cherche à agresser Lucy ?

Pour le savoir, coche la bonne réponse.

Quelle question Lucy remue-t-elle dans sa tête durant toute cette journée ?

- **a.** Elle est sûre que Jeremy a continué sans elle. . . . . . ☐
- **b.** Elle se demande s'il n'a pas besoin d'elle. . . . . ☐

➡ LIS LE CORRIGÉ DU N° 4 PAGE 64.

Combien de temps s'est-il passé depuis le début de l'aventure ? Recopie les mots du paragraphe qui l'indiquent :

C'est ton SIXIÈME INDICE.

N'oublie pas de le noter sur ta page-indices page 95.

PARLER D'ÉVENTUALITÉ

La mère de Lucy pense que sa fille est peut-être malade.

Quelle est la phrase où elle dit cela ?

a. You're very pale. **b.** You might be ill.

Tu as répondu a ➡ VA VOIR LE N° 4.
Tu as répondu b ➡ VA VOIR LE N° 7.

mémo 20

Corrigé des questions de compréhension

1

1. a. Que l'on puisse dépenser de l'argent pour un serpent.
'People pay for snakes!' I exclaimed.

2. a. Dans le garage de la villa.
'The garage is empty', I said, 'you could sleep there.'

2

1. b. Elle reconnaît son accent.
I recognized that voice, that South American accent!

2. b. Elle l'avait trouvé très agréable.
He was very charming.

3

1. b. Elle pense que son père n'apprécierait pas d'avoir des inconnus chez lui.
I don't think he would like strange men in the house.

2. a. Elle ne retrouve pas Jeremy dans le garage.
The garage was empty!

4

b. Elle se demande s'il n'a pas besoin d'elle.
...perhaps he needed me.

Lucy in action

1 

Where were the stones coming from? When I looked at the restaurant, the avalanche stopped.
'Psst! Lucy, I'm here', whispered a familiar voice.
Jeremy! He wasn't on the yacht, he was hiding behind the restaurant!
'I'm so pleased to see you!' I exclaimed. 'I was worried*. Why did you leave the garage?'
'Did you see the man who was talking to your mother?' he asked.
'Yes', I answered. 'I recognized his voice.'
'He came[4] to your house with a woman', he continued. 'He distracted* your mother and the woman came into the garage. Someone saw[27] us last night because this woman knew[17] I was there. I wasn't

worried : inquiète
distract : détourner l'attention de

sleeping, so I was able to escape. I'm hiding here because I can't go anywhere. They're looking for me, Lucy. I need your help, more than ever*!'

De quelle manière Lucy va-t-elle pouvoir l'aider ?

Pour le découvrir, coche la bonne réponse.
Qu'est-ce que Jeremy a découvert ?

a. L'homme à l'accent connaissait la mère de Lucy. . . . ☐
b. Cet homme était avec une femme qui savait que Jeremy était dans le garage. ☐

→ LIS LE CORRIGÉ N° 1 PAGE 74.

PARLER DE CAPACITÉ

Lorsque Jeremy raconte qu'il « a pu » s'échapper, il dit : 'I was able to escape'.

À quel temps est cette phrase ?

a. au présent **b.** au passé

Tu as répondu a → VA VOIR LE N° 4.
Tu as répondu b → VA VOIR LE N° 6.

mémo 13

2 

Faux. En disant 'What about seeing if there's a window open?', *Lucy ne suggère pas à Jeremy de regarder « par la fenêtre », mais de regarder s'il y a une fenêtre ouverte.* → *Lis le n° 8.*

more than ever: plus que jamais

3

Suddenly, at 5 o'clock, the door opened and three people came out. There was Jack, the man with the accent and a woman, who was wearing dark glasses and a bandana. She was carrying a bag. I followed them. They walked towards the hills* and after twenty minutes, they stopped at the door of a small fisherman's cottage*. The woman unlocked* the door and they all went in. Jeremy was right again. They had a house in the town! I ran[25] to the restaurant where he was hiding and told[37] him everything.

'Excellent,' he said, 'let's go'.

We found[9] a place to hide near the cottage. After a few minutes, the three people came[4] out, locked the door and walked towards the harbour.

'They haven't got the bag', I whispered.

We waited another ten minutes before approaching* the house.

'Lucy,' said Jeremy, 'you know how to *escape* from a locked room, but do you know how to *enter* one?'

a hill : une colline
a fisherman's cottage : la cabane d'un pêcheur
unlock : ouvrir (la serrure d'une porte)
before approaching : avant de nous approcher

'What about seeing if there's a window open?' I suggested.

We examined the windows but they were all shut.

Quel moyen vont-ils trouver pour entrer dans la cabane ?

Pour le savoir, coche les deux bonnes réponses.
Que découvre Lucy ?

1 **a.** Elle voit Jack sortir du yacht avec deux personnes. . ☐
b. Elle voit seulement sortir une femme avec un sac. . . ☐

2 **a.** Elle voit la femme frapper à la porte d'une cabane de pêcheur. . . . . ☐
b. Elle voit cette femme ouvrir la cabane avec sa clé. . ☐

→ LIS LE CORRIGÉ N° 3 PAGE 74.

FAIRE DES SUGGESTIONS

Lucy dit : 'What about seeing if there's a window open?'

Quelle est la bonne traduction de sa question ?

a. Que dirais-tu de regarder par la fenêtre ?
b. Et si on regardait s'il y a une fenêtre ouverte ?

Tu as répondu a → VA VOIR LE N° 2.
Tu as répondu b → VA VOIR LE N° 8.

mémo 21

4 

Faux, la phrase est au passé, comme l'indique was *(forme du singulier du prétérit de* be*).* 'I was able to escape' = *Je pus / réussis à m'échapper.* → *Lis le n° 6.*

5

Bonne réponse ! → *Va maintenant au chapitre 8.*

6

'What can I do?' I asked.

'First,' he answered, 'you need to change your appearance. We're not sure if they know you, but they might have a description. Put on a big hat, some sunglasses and change your clothes. Then you must watch the yacht…'

'… But it's not there,' I interrupted.

'They'll come back', said Jeremy, 'my uncle often goes out to sea when he has "business" to do. If you see someone leaving the yacht, you must follow them. I'm sure that the criminals also have a house in the town. The computer might be in the house. So, we must find the computer, print* the page and take it to the police.'

---

print : imprimer

'And you?' I asked, 'what are you going to do?'
'I'll wait here', he answered. 'When you know where the house is, come here and tell me.'
I went home, changed my clothes and went[13] back to the harbour. Jeremy was right, the yacht was coming back. I sat[30] in the park and watched it. One hour passed… nothing. Two hours… I was hungry and bored*, James Bond girls didn't do these things!

La patience de Lucy sera-t-elle récompensée ?

Pour le savoir, coche les deux bonnes réponses.

1 Quelle mission Jeremy confie-t-il à Lucy ?

a. Prendre les gens du yacht en filature. . . . . ☐
b. Faire le guet devant la villa des parents. . . . . ☐

2 Quel est le plan de Jeremy ?

a. Apporter l'ordinateur à la police. . . . . ☐
b. Fournir à la police la page compromettante. . . . . ☐

➡ Lis le corrigé n° 2 page 74.

PARLER D'ÉVENTUALITÉ

En parlant de l'ordinateur, Jeremy dit à Lucy : 'The computer might be in the house.'

Que veut-il dire par là ?

a. Il n'est pas du tout sûr qu'il soit dans la maison.
b. Il est certain qu'il est dans la maison.

Tu as répondu a ➡ Va voir le n° 3.
Tu as répondu b ➡ Va voir le n° 9.

mémo 20

I was bored : je m'ennuyais

7 

Tu t'es trompé(e). Lucy raconte ce qui leur restait, à ce moment-là, à faire : 'We had to go to the police.' = *Il fallait qu'on aille à la police.* → *Va au chapitre 8.*

8 

Jeremy took[36] a stone in his hand, 'It's easy...,' he began[3].

'No', I said, 'someone will hear the noise'. I was pushing the windows, one by one.

'Yes!' I exclaimed, 'the bathroom window isn't completely closed.'

It was not a big window. Again not very elegantly, I went head first into the bathroom... and I found myself looking into a toilet! Jeremy pushed my feet. I stood[34] up and went into the lounge where I opened a bigger window for Jeremy. Together* we examined the lounge.

'Yes!' exclaimed Jeremy suddenly, 'Lucy, here it is... the computer!'

Jeremy switched it on. PASSWORD?

'P-E-T-E-R', he wrote[41]. PASSWORD ACCEPTED.

I saw the bag and opened it. It was full of money, thousands of dollars.

---

together : ensemble

'Operation Blue Lagoon', murmured Jeremy. 'Print!'

Five minutes later, we had the papers. I wanted to leave quickly. I closed the lounge window behind Jeremy and was starting to climb out of the bathroom, when he suddenly said[26], 'Wait, Lucy, there's one more thing I must do.'

'What!' I exclaimed, 'Are you crazy? They could come back and find us here!'

'I'm sorry, Lucy', he insisted. 'Open the window for me again. Please! You watch the street.'

Five minutes passed. 'Jeremy, what are you doing? We must go!' I said.

'Okay', he answered. 'Thanks for waiting*. We can go now.'

I climbed out of the bathroom window and we were in the street again. We had the papers and now we had to go to the police!

thanks for waiting : merci d'avoir attendu

Ces papiers suffiront-ils pour convaincre la police ?

Pour le découvrir, coche la bonne réponse.
Nos deux héros ont-ils trouvé ce qu'ils cherchaient ?

a. Les trois complices avaient caché l'ordinateur dans la cabane. . . . . ☐

b. Ils étaient repartis avec l'argent de la contrebande. ☐

➡ LIS LE CORRIGÉ N° 4 PAGE 74.

Recopie le nom de code du trafic qui permet de gagner des milliers de dollars :

C'est ton SEPTIÈME INDICE.
N'oublie pas de le noter sur ta page-indices page 95.

PARLER D'OBLIGATION

Lucy dit : 'we had to go to the police.'

Quelle est la bonne traduction de cette phrase ?

a. Il fallait qu'on aille à la police.

b. Il a fallu qu'on aille à la police.

Tu as répondu a ➡ VA VOIR LE N° 5.
Tu as répondu b ➡ VA VOIR LE N° 7.

mémo 18

9 

Mauvaise réponse. Avec might, *Jeremy exprime une éventualité et non une certitude. En disant à propos de l'ordinateur* 'The computer might be in the house.', *il n'est pas du tout sûr qu'il soit dans la maison.* → *Lis le n° 3.*

Corrigé des questions de compréhension

1

b. Cet homme était avec une femme qui savait que Jeremy était dans le garage.

Someone saw us last night because this woman knew I was there.

2

1. a. Prendre les gens du yacht en filature.

If you see someone leaving the yacht, you must follow them.

2. b. Fournir à la police la page compromettante.

We must (...) print the page and take it to the police.

3

1. a. Elle voit Jack sortir du yacht avec deux personnes.

There was Jack, the man with the accent and a woman.

2. b. Elle voit cette femme ouvrir la cabane avec sa clé.

The woman unlocked the door.

4

a. Les trois complices avaient caché l'ordinateur dans la cabane.

Lucy, here it is... the computer!

8

Fire!

1

Night was falling when we arrived at the police station.

'We would like to see a police officer', Jeremy announced to one of the two policemen at reception. I looked at his badge: 'Sergeant Ricks'.

'You're looking at one now', he answered, without any trace of humour. 'What's the problem?'

Jeremy hesitated. This wasn't going to be easy*.

'I found[9] some information on my uncle's computer. He knows some reptile smugglers. I have a list of names.'

The sergeant looked incredulous. 'What's your name, boy?' he asked.

'Jeremy Robinson,' answered Jeremy.

---

this wasn't going to be easy : ça n'allait pas être facile

'Ah, *Jeremy Robinson!*' he exclaimed, 'The boy who disappeared from the yacht! We spent[33] a lot of time looking for you, you know...'

'Yes, I know. I'm sorry. But now I have important information for you. Look at this...'

He gave[12] the list of names to the sergeant.

'Operation Blue Lagoon!' he said, laughing, 'Listen, Charlie', he said to his colleague, 'Operation Blue Lagoon!'

The second policeman smiled and continued reading his newspaper. The sergeant's face became[2] serious again.

'Listen, my boy', he said, 'I think that you read too many adventure books. Take your list, take your girlfriend, go home and stop wasting our time*.'

stop wasting our time : arrête de nous faire perdre notre temps

Quelqu'un va-t-il quand même croire Jeremy ?

Pour le savoir, coche les deux bonnes réponses.

Comment Lucy et Jeremy sont-ils reçus au commissariat ?

1 **a.** Le brigadier Ricks ne croit pas Jeremy. . . . . ☐
b. Il n'avait jamais entendu parler de lui. . . . . ☐
2 **a.** Ricks prend ensuite leur histoire au sérieux.. . . . . . . ☐
b. Ricks finit par se fâcher. . . . . ☐

→ LIS LE CORRIGÉ DU N° 1 PAGE 86.

CONTINUER À FAIRE QUELQUE CHOSE

Quelle est la bonne traduction de cette phrase ?

'He continued reading his newspaper.'
a. Il continua à lire son journal.
b. Il continua à écrire sur son journal.

Tu as répondu a → VA VOIR LE N° 6.
Tu as répondu b → VA VOIR LE N° 7.

mémo 7

2

Mauvaise réponse. Employé après if (only), could *(prétérit de* can*) n'exprime pas le passé, mais une situation imaginaire : « si on pouvait ».* 'If only we could find the reptiles!' = *Si seulement on pouvait trouver les reptiles ! → Lis le n° 9.*

3

Faux. Avec le modal will + have to, *Jeremy dit ce qu'ils « auront » à faire (obligation dans le futur).* 'I

suppose we'll have to go back to the cottage.' =*Je suppose qu'il faudra qu'on retourne à la cabane.* → *Lis le n° 4.*

4

'Don't scream', repeated the man. 'I want to help you, okay?'

I nodded* and he took[36] away* his hand. Jeremy was furious again.

'Who are you?' he exclaimed. 'Why were you following us?'

nod : faire signe que oui
take away : retirer

'Jeremy, I know who he is', I said, 'it's the other policeman.'
'My name's Charlie Brooks', said the man. 'I'm sorry about my colleague, but you see, a lot of kids tell us stories. It's not his fault.'
Okay, I thought[38], you're a policeman, but we're not in a gangster movie and it is possible to introduce yourself* normally in the street. But I didn't say anything.
'I know that Operation Blue Lagoon exists', Brooks continued, 'and I was following Jack Robinson. Please, can I see your list?'
Jeremy gave him the list. Brooks looked at it and whistled*.
'The clients!' he exclaimed. 'If only we could find the reptiles, then I would have enough evidence*...'
'Yes, yes!' exclaimed Jeremy, 'the snakes are in cages on the yacht!'
I suddenly saw[27] something and closed my eyes. Was I dreaming? I opened them again. No, it was true. I was looking towards the harbour... and I could see flames and smoke. I knew what was burning...

introduce yourself : vous présenter
whistle : siffler
evidence : des preuves

Arriveront-ils à temps pour éteindre l'incendie ?

Pour le savoir, coche les deux bonnes réponses.

1 Pourquoi le brigadier Brooks les rejoint-il ?

a. Il veut seulement s'excuser pour son collègue. . . . . ☐

b. Il veut en savoir plus sur l'affaire « Blue Lagoon » qu'il suit. . . . . ☐

2 Comment Lucy trouve-t-elle la façon dont Brooks l'a abordée ?

a. Elle se dit que l'on peut tout de même se comporter plus correctement. . . . . ☐

b. La scène l'a autant amusée qu'un film de gangster.. ☐

➡ LIS LE CORRIGÉ N° 3 PAGE 86.

EXPRIMER UN REGRET

Lorsque Brooks regrette de ne pas avoir assez de preuves, il dit : 'If only we could find the reptiles!'

Quelle est la bonne traduction de cette phrase ?

a. Si seulement on avait trouvé les reptiles !

b. Si seulement on pouvait trouver les reptiles !

Tu as répondu a ➡ VA VOIR LE N° 2.
Tu as répondu b ➡ VA VOIR LE N° 9.

mémo 15

5

Excellent ! Va vite lire le n° 10 pour savoir ce qui attend nos deux héros !

6

We left[19] the police station. Jeremy was furious.

'Did you see his expression?' he asked. 'He didn't believe a word of my story. Not a word! Lucy, I'm going to take one of those snakes from the yacht, a poisonous snake, and I'm going to put it in his...'

'Jeremy', I interrupted, 'I don't think we can walk through the centre of the town carrying a poisonous snake!'

We looked at each other* and began[3] to laugh.

'Sorry', said Jeremy, 'but I hate it when adults think that young people can't do anything serious. If your parents came[4] to the police station with us, I'm sure that Sergeant Ricks would believe us immediately...'

'I don't think that's a good idea', I said quickly.

The streets were empty, but I had the impression that someone was behind us. When I looked, nobody was there.

'What do we do now?' I asked.

'Good question', answered Jeremy, 'I suppose we'll have to go back to the cottage and...'

He didn't finish his sentence. A man came out of the shadows*, put his hand over my mouth and whispered in my ear 'Don't scream'.

---

we looked at each other : nous nous regardâmes
the shadows : l'obscurité

Quel est cet homme et que leur veut-il ?

Pour le savoir, coche les deux bonnes réponses.

1 Comment Jeremy réagit-il aux paroles du brigadier Ricks ?

a. Il est sûr que Ricks finira par les croire. . . . . ☐
b. Il a l'intention de jouer un mauvais tour à Ricks. . . . ☐

2 Qu'arrive-t-il soudain à Lucy ?

a. Lucy se met à crier en voyant surgir quelqu'un. . . . ☐
b. Lucy ne se sent pas tranquille dans cette rue. . . . . . ☐

→ LIS LE CORRIGÉ N° 2 PAGE 86.

PARLER D'OBLIGATION

Lorsque Jeremy dit 'I suppose we'll have to go back to the cottage', **qu'exprime-t-il ?**

a. une obligation dans le passé
b. une obligation dans le futur

Tu as répondu a → VA VOIR LE N° 3.
Tu as répondu b → VA VOIR LE N° 4.

mémo 19

7

Faux. 'He continued reading his newspaper'*: Lucy explique que le deuxième brigadier continua, non pas à écrire, mais à lire son journal.* → *Lis le n° 6.*

8

Faux. Lucy raconte ici ce qui se passa réellement : '...that they couldn't go near.' = *...qu'ils ne purent pas approcher.* → *Va lire maintenant le n° 10.*

9

We ran to the harbour. The sirens of the fire engines became[2] louder and louder. The yacht was on fire. Curious people came to watch, but the heat* was so intense that they couldn't go near. A cloud of black smoke was forming in the night sky. It was clear that nothing and nobody could be saved. I took Jeremy's hand, he was shaking. Everything that he possessed was on that yacht. I read[24] his thoughts* : 'Jack wasn't on the yacht', I whispered, 'I'm sure'. Brooks put his head in his hands.

'The evidence!' he exclaimed. 'I can't do anything with a list of names on paper!'

Jeremy looked at him, hesitated and put his hand in his pocket. He showed me a disk.

'The complete file*?' I asked. 'Did you make a copy when you went back inside the cottage?'

'Yes, and yes' he answered.

'Sergeant Brooks', said Jeremy, 'will this help?'

the heat : la chaleur
his thoughts : ses pensées
a file : un fichier (dans un ordinateur)

Cette incroyable affaire va-t-elle être résolue ?

Pour le découvrir, coche la bonne réponse.

Qu'avait fait Jeremy du fichier compromettant ?

a. Il en avait fait une copie sur le bateau. . . . . ☐
b. Il était retourné dans la cabane pour en faire une copie. . ☐

➡ LIS LE CORRIGÉ N° 4 PAGE 86.

Recopie la phrase qui dit que le bateau est en flammes.

C'est ton DERNIER INDICE.
N'oublie pas de le noter sur ta page-indices page 95.

PARLER D'INCAPACITÉ

Quelle est la bonne traduction des mots soulignés ?

'The heat was so intense that they couldn't go near.'

a. si intense qu'ils ne purent approcher.
b. si intense qu'ils ne pourraient pas approcher.

Tu as répondu a ➡ VA VOIR LE N° 5.
Tu as répondu b ➡ VA VOIR LE N° 8.

mémo 14

10

That was the end of our adventure. The police went to the cottage but there was no trace of the computer or the money. But with the information on Jeremy's disk, the police were able to stop the reptile smuggling and arrest Jack's associates. They examined the yacht and confirmed that no people and no animals died in the fire. What happened to Uncle Jack? Did he escape with the reptiles? The only thing we know is that he disappeared on the night of the fire. Was he a criminal or was he simply a victim of circumstances? We don't know and we'll probably never know.

And Jeremy, I hear you ask. What happened to Jeremy? Soon after the fire, he went[4] to live with a family on the island. I finally explained to my parents who he was and gave[12] them a version (simplified!) of our adventure. Jeremy and I spent every day of the last week of my holiday together and then we e-mailed each other during the winter. Then, my parents found[9] him a place in a school here in London and he's going to live near us.

The plane is now here and the first people are beginning to arrive. He's here! I can't believe it! Jeremy! Jeremy…!

THE END

Bravo ! Puisque tu es allé(e) jusqu'au bout de cette histoire et de ses exercices, nous te proposons de nous envoyer, sur le site www.lenigme.com, la liste des indices que tu as écrits page 95 et tu pourras télécharger des surprises !

À bientôt, pour une nouvelle aventure !

Corrigé des questions de compréhension

1

1. a. Le brigadier Ricks ne croit pas Jeremy.
The sergeant looked incredulous.

2. b. Ricks finit par se fâcher.
Stop wasting our time.

2

1. b. Il a l'intention de jouer un mauvais tour à Ricks.
I'm going to take one of those snakes from the yacht, a poisonous snake, and I'm going to put it in his…

2. b. Lucy ne se sent pas tranquille dans cette rue.
I had the impression that someone was behind us.

3

1. b. Il veut en savoir plus sur l'affaire « Blue Lagoon » qu'il suit.
I was following Jack Robinson. Please, can I see your list?

2. a. Elle se dit que l'on peut tout de même se comporter plus correctement.
… it is possible to introduce yourself normally in the street.

4

b. Il était retourné dans la cabane pour en faire une copie.
'The complete file?' (…) 'Did you make a copy when you went back inside the cottage?' 'Yes, and yes.'

Mémento pour t'aider

FAIRE DES COMPARAISONS

1 Le comparatif de supériorité

La construction du comparatif de supériorité dépend de la longueur de l'adjectif :
• ***-er*** ajouté à un adjectif court (1 ou 2 syllabes) :
He's a little older than me. (Il est un peu plus âgé que moi.)
• ***more*** devant un adjectif long (2 syllabes ou plus) :
This model is more expensive. (Ce modèle est plus cher.)
Than introduit le 2e élément de la comparaison.

2 Le superlatif de supériorité

La construction du superlatif de supériorité dépend de la longueur de l'adjectif :
• ***-est*** ajouté à un adjectif court :
one of the biggest yachts (un des plus grands yachts)
• ***the most*** devant un adjectif long :
the most expensive yacht (le yacht le plus cher)

RACONTER AU PASSÉ

3 Raconter au prétérit

Pour raconter au passé, on utilise le prétérit, qui peut être employé seul (prétérit simple) :
• ***-ed*** est la marque du prétérit des verbes réguliers.
The days passed. (Les jours passèrent.)
Pour les verbes irréguliers, voir la liste page 94.
• Le prétérit peut être aussi associé avec ***be -ing***.
One year ago I was waiting for the plane.
(Il y a un an, j'attendais l'avion.)
L'emploi de *was* (prétérit singulier de *be*) + verbe avec *-ing* permet de décrire une activité qui était en train de se dérouler.

4 Raconter au plus-que-parfait

On peut aussi raconter au passé en utilisant, comme en français, un plus-que-parfait :
auxiliaire ***have* au prétérit + verbe au participe passé**
He had found a piece of the puzzle. (Il avait trouvé une pièce du puzzle.)
Le plus-que-parfait permet de parler d'une action achevée à un moment donné du récit.

Exprimer l'étonnement

5 Pour exprimer l'étonnement, on utilise souvent, comme en français, la forme interro-**négative**. On n'attend pas alors, vraiment, une réponse. Comparons :
Did you know that? (Savais-tu ça ?) ➥ « vraie » question
*Did**n't** you know?* (Ne le savais-tu pas ?) ➥ « je m'étonne »
They locked the door, Lucy, didn't you know? ➥ En fait, Jeremy se doute bien qu'elle est au courant !

Parler de fréquence

6 À la différence du français, les adverbes de fréquence – comme *often* (souvent), *always* (toujours), etc. – se placent en anglais **avant le verbe**.
My uncle often leaves me alone. (Mon oncle me laisse souvent seul.)
Exception : les adverbes de fréquence se placent **après le verbe *be***!
Jeremy is often alone. (Jeremy est souvent seul.)

Continuer et s'arrêter

7 Continuer à faire quelque chose

Le verbe ***continue*** + verbe avec ***-ing*** signifie « continuer à faire quelque chose ».
He continued reading. (Il continua à lire.)
Reading est ici le complément d'objet du verbe *continue*, et fonctionne donc comme un nom (« la lecture »).

8 S'arrêter de faire quelque chose

Le verbe ***stop*** + verbe avec ***-ing*** signifie « s'arrêter de faire quelque chose ».
He stopped smoking. (Il s'est arrêté de fumer.)
Smoking est ici le complément d'objet du verbe *stop*, et fonctionne donc comme un nom (« la cigarette »).

Exprimer le conditionnel

9 En anglais, il n'y a pas de mode conditionnel.
Pour exprimer le conditionnel, on emploie le plus souvent le modal ***would*** + base verbale.
If I went out of the front door, my parents would wake up. (Si je sortais par la porte d'entrée, mes parents se réveilleraient.)

Exprimer un désir

10 Pour exprimer un désir, on emploie :
- modal ***would*** + verbe ***like*** + ***to*** + **base verbale**

I would like to go to the cinema. (J'aimerais aller au cinéma.)
- modal ***would*** + verbe ***like*** + **nom**

I would like a cup of tea. (J'aimerais une tasse de thé.)

Parler de possibilité

11 **Parler de possibilité au passé**
Pour raconter au passé ce que « l'on pouvait » faire (ou non), on emploie ***could***, qui est le prétérit du modal *can*.
I can't go there. (Je ne peux pas y aller.) ➥ présent
I couldn't go there. (Je ne pouvais pas y aller.) ➥ passé

12 **Parler de possibilité au conditionnel**
Pour dire au conditionnel ce que « l'on pourrait » faire, ou « ce qui pourrait » arriver, on peut employer le modal *could*.
If the police catch them, it could save my uncle. (…, cela pourrait sauver mon oncle.)

Parler de capacité et d'incapacité

13 **Parler de capacité au passé**
Pour raconter au passé ce que « l'on a pu » faire, on emploie fréquemment l'expression *be able to* (être capable de) au prétérit : ***was able to*** (singulier) et ***were able to*** (pluriel).
I was able to escape. (J'ai pu / réussi à m'échapper.)
They were able to stop the smugglers. (Ils réussirent à arrêter les contrebandiers.)
Attention ! Dans ce sens-là, l'emploi de *could* est impossible.

14 Parler d'incapacité au passé

Pour raconter ce que « l'on n'a pas pu » faire, on peut employer au choix :

• ***was not able to*** (singulier) et ***were not able to*** (pluriel)

He wasn't able to mend his bike. (Il n'a pas réussi à réparer son vélo.)

• ***couldn't*** (modal *could* + *not*)

The heat was so intense that they couldn't go near.
(La chaleur était si intense qu'ils n'ont pas pu approcher.)

Exprimer un regret

15 On peut exprimer un regret à l'aide de ***If only*** + **prétérit** :

If only I had a moped! (Si seulement j'avais une mobylette !)

Ici, le prétérit n'évoque pas une situation passée, mais une situation imaginaire ➥ « si j'avais » car, en réalité, « je n'en ai pas ».

If only we could find the reptiles! (Si seulement on pouvait trouver les reptiles !)

Could (prétérit de *can*) évoque de même une situation imaginaire ➥ « si on pouvait » car, en réalité, « on ne peut pas ».

Exprimer le futur

16 En anglais, il n'y a pas de temps grammatical futur.

Pour exprimer le futur, on peut employer :

• le présent avec ***be -ing***

I'm leaving tomorrow. (Je pars demain.)

Avec la forme *be -ing*, on décrit à l'avance l'activité prévue.

• le modal ***will*** + base verbale

Perhaps you will see someone. (Tu verras peut-être quelqu'un.)

➥ Lucy fait ici un pari : peut-être bien que ça arrivera.

I'll write them later. (Je les écrirai plus tard.) ➥ Lucy décide ici, en parlant, de ce qu'elle fera.

Will se dit le plus souvent sous une forme contractée : « *'ll* ».

• l'expression ***be going to***

I'm going to switch off the computer. (Je vais éteindre l'ordinateur.)

Avec *be going to*, le locuteur annonce une décision déjà prise.

Parler d'obligation

17 Parler d'obligation au présent

• On emploie le modal ***must*** + base verbale lorsque l'obligation est imposée par quelqu'un.

We must find the information on the computer. (Il faut qu'on trouve…) ➥ C'est Jeremy qui juge « qu'il le faut ».

• ***Must*** + **négation** marque l'interdiction.
My uncle says that I must never try to go in. (… je ne dois jamais essayer d'entrer.) ➥ C'est l'oncle qui dit « qu'il ne faut pas ».
• On emploie ***have to*** + base verbale lorsque l'obligation est due aux circonstances.
I still have to do my schoolwork. (Il faut quand même que je fasse mes devoirs.) ➥ Même en vivant sur un bateau, il faut bien étudier !

18 Parler d'obligation au passé

Pour exprimer une obligation dans le passé, on emploie ***have to*** **au prétérit**. Le passé est exprimé par ***had***, prétérit de *have*.
I had to think of something different. (Il fallait que je pense…)

19 Parler d'obligation au futur

Pour exprimer une obligation dans le futur, on emploie ***will*** + ***have to***. Le futur est exprimé par le modal *will*.
I suppose we'll have to go back there. (Je suppose qu'il faudra qu'on y retourne.)

Parler d'éventualité

20 Pour donner un avis sur quelque chose dont il n'est pas très sûr (quelque chose qui « pourrait arriver »), le locuteur emploie très souvent les modaux ***may*** ou ***might*** + base verbale.
I think you might be ill. (Je crois que tu es peut-être malade.)
It may be the heat. (C'est peut-être la chaleur.)

Faire des suggestions

21 Il y a plusieurs manières de suggérer quelque chose :
• ***Let's*** + base verbale ➥ *Let's go in.* (Entrons.)
Avec *let's*, le locuteur « pousse » autrui à faire quelque chose avec lui.
• Modal ***could*** + base verbale ➥ *You could sleep there.* (Tu pourrais dormir là.)
Avec *could*, qui a ici un sens de conditionnel, le locuteur donne son avis : la chose suggérée lui « paraît possible ».
• ***What about*** + **V-*ing***
What about seeing if there's a window open?
(Et si on regardait s'il y a une fenêtre ouverte ?)
Ici, le locuteur fait « imaginer » l'activité suggérée : dans cet exemple, observer les fenêtres.

Table des matières

Verbes irréguliers

	base verbale	prétérit	participe passé	traduction
1	**be**	was *(sing.)* were *(pluriel)*	been	*être*
2	**become**	became	become	*devenir*
3	**begin**	began	begun	*commencer*
4	**come**	came	come	*venir*
5	**do**	did	done	*faire*
6	**drink**	drank	drunk	*boire*
7	**fall**	fell	fallen	*tomber*
8	**feel**	felt	felt	*se sentir*
9	**find**	found	found	*trouver*
10	**forget**	forgot	forgotten	*oublier*
11	**get**	got	got	*aller chercher* get up : *se lever*
12	**give**	gave	given	*donner*
13	**go**	went	gone	*aller*
14	**have**	had	had	*avoir, prendre (un repas)*
15	**hear**	heard	heard	*entendre*
16	**hit**	hit	hit	*frapper*
17	**know**	knew	known	*savoir*
18	**leap**	leapt	leapt	*bondir*
19	**leave**	left	left	*quitter, laisser*
20	**make**	made	made	*faire*
21	**meet**	met	met	*rencontrer, se retrouver*
22	**pay**	paid	paid	*payer*
23	**put**	put	put	*mettre, poser*
24	**read**	read	read	*lire*
25	**run**	ran	run	*courir*
26	**say**	said	said	*dire*
27	**see**	saw	seen	*voir*
28	**shine**	shone	shone	*briller*
29	**shut**	shut	shut	*fermer*
30	**sit**	sat	sat	*s'asseoir* sit down : *s'asseoir*
31	**slide**	slid	slid	*glisser*
32	**speak**	spoke	spoken	*parler*
33	**spend**	spent	spent	*passer (du temps)*
34	**stand**	stood	stood	*être debout* stand up : *se lever*
35	**swim**	swam	swum	*nager*
36	**take**	took	taken	*prendre*
37	**tell**	told	told	*dire, raconter*
38	**think**	thought	thought	*penser*
39	**throw**	threw	thrown	*lancer, jeter*
40	**wake**	woke	woken	wake up : *se réveiller*
41	**write**	wrote	written	*écrire*

Page-indices

Operation Blue Lagoon

de la 5ᵉ à la 4ᵉ

Note ci-dessous les indices que tu as trouvés au cours de ta lecture.

Va vite te connecter sur le site

www.lenigme.com

pour nous envoyer tes indices, et tu pourras télécharger plein de

Cadeaux !

Indice 1 : ....

Indice 2 : ....

Indice 3 : ....

Indice 4 : ....

Indice 5 : ....

Indice 6 : ....

Indice 7 : ....

Indice 8 : ....

Bravo ! Tu as trouvé tous les indices ! Pour finir, dis en anglais en quoi consiste *Operation Blue Lagoon* :

....

Tourne la page !

IMPRIM'VERT

N° d'éditeur : 10182073 - C2000 - Mars 2012 - Imprimé en France par I.M.E.

La collection

L'ÉNIGME des vacances

Choisis ton univers !

Historique · Fantastique · Policier · Aventure · Frisson · Princesse · Sciences

du CP au CE1
- Le voleur invisible
- Sophia, princesse de la mer
- Le mystère de la source

du CE1 au CE2
- La peur au bout de la laisse
- Mystère au cirque Alzared
- Attention ! Dauphins en danger
- Pas si désert que ça !
- Menace sur Madagascar
- Pirates en péril !

du CE2 au CM1
- Le labyrinthe des dragons
- Les fantômes de Glamorgan
- La plage du Prince Blanc
- Le phare de la peur
- Montagne explosive !
- Menaces sur la finale de foot

du CM1 au CM2
- Le voleur de papyrus (iPhone iPad)
- L'œil de feu
- Le sortilège de la pleine lune
- Parfum de vacances
- La carrière interdite
- Feu mystérieux en Australie

du CM2 à la 6e
- Le trésor des Templiers
- Panique à la Pop Academy
- La forêt de l'épouvante
- À la recherche de la cité perdue (iPhone iPad)
- Eaux troubles à Venise

de la 6e à la 5e
- Le secret du Titanic (iPhone iPad)
- Drôle de trafic
- La cinquième fourchette

de la 5e à la 4e
- *Operation Blue Lagoon* (en anglais)
- Le saut de l'ange (iPhone iPad)
- *The Captain is Missing!* (en anglais)

de la 4e à la 3e
- *Murder in West Park* (en anglais)
- *The Mark of the Vampire* (en anglais) (iPhone iPad)

Histoire à podcaster sur le site www.lenigme.com

iPhone iPad Existe en applications pour iPhone et iPad. Disponible sur App Store.

Retrouve-nous sur le site : www.lenigme.com